HERE COME *the* Bears

by Alice Goudey

illustrated by Garry MacKenzie

Purple House Press
Kentucky

We are grateful to Lee S. Crandall,
General Curator Emeritus of the New York Zoological Society
for reading and checking the text of this book.

Prior to 1975, Alaskan brown bears and grizzly bears were considered to be separate species. Now it's known that they are the same, *Ursus arctos*, but that grizzly bears are a subspecies, *Ursus arctos horribilis*, of brown bears.

Even though grizzlies are a subspecies, the difference between a grizzly bear and a brown bear is fairly arbitrary. In North America, brown bears are generally considered to be those of the species that have access to coastal food resources like salmon. Grizzly bears live further inland and typically do not have access to marine-derived food resources.

Besides habitat and diet, there are physical differences between brown and grizzly bears. Large male brown bears in Katmai, Alaska, can routinely weigh over 1000 pounds in the fall. In contrast, grizzly bears in Yellowstone National Park weigh far less on average. There have been no documented cases of grizzly bears weighing over 900 pounds in Yellowstone.

—US National Park Services

Published by
Purple House Press
PO Box 787
Cynthiana, Kentucky 41031

Classic Books for Kids and Young Adults
purplehousepress.com

Written in 1954 by Alice Goudey.
Text is slightly revised. Illustrations recolored.
Copyright © 2021 by Purple House Press.
ISBN 9781948959469
All rights reserved.

THE GRIZZLY BEARS

THE GRIZZLY BEARS

Two furry little Grizzly Bears peek out of their den high in the Rocky Mountains.

It is the first time they have seen the outside world.

Patches of snow lie upon the mountainside. But the sun is warm, the sky is blue and tiny blades of grass can be seen here and there.

The little cubs whimper and cry for their mother even though they can see her just outside the den.

Mother Grizzly Bear rears up on her hind legs and sniffs the air.

It is spring and she is hungry.

She has been sleeping and dozing in her den all winter. But she did not sleep as soundly as a woodchuck does. She is a light sleeper. She would have awakened if a hunter had entered the den.

She has had no food or water since she went to sleep. She did not store food in her den to eat during the winter as squirrels do. She stored *her* food in her own body.

Before she went to sleep she ate acorns and beechnuts, mice, berries and many other things until her sides grew fat and round.

She ate so much that she did not need another bite of food for four months.

Now Mother Grizzly Bear is hungry for the young green grass, the tender ferns and the skunk cabbage roots that are growing where the snow has melted.

She is very thirsty. She drinks some water made by the melting snow which she finds in a hollow place in a rock.

Mother Grizzly Bear is a large shaggy creature with a big head and a dished face. She belongs to the "dish-faced" bear family.

She has small eyes for such a large animal. She has little rounded ears and a funny stump of a tail. She has a hump on her shoulders which makes her look different from her cousins, the Black Bears.

Her shaggy coat is dark brown. Many of the hairs are tipped with a whitish-silvery color. This is the reason she is sometimes called Silvertip.

Brother Cub is dark brown like his mother. Sister Cub, who is smaller than her brother, has a pale yellow coat.

Brother and Sister were born in their snug den in January.

How tiny they were!

They did not weigh as much as a pound of butter. Mother Grizzly Bear could have covered one of them with her huge paw.

When they were born they had no hair, they had no teeth and their eyes were shut, as a newborn kitten's are. They snuggled in their mother's shaggy fur to keep warm. They drank her rich milk when they were hungry.

Their eyes opened when they were about six weeks old, and before long their fat little bodies were covered with soft furry coats of their own. Now they have teeth that are as sharp as needles. Already they would make rough playmates.

One sunny day Mother Grizzly Bear decides it is time for the cubs to leave their home grounds. She gives a soft coaxing grunt which seems to say, "Come with me."

This is to be a day of great adventure.

But first the little cubs want to play. They roll over and over on the ground trying to chew each other's ears.

They stand up and box.

They play tag until Brother crawls up on a big stone. Sister is too small for such a big climb.

Mother makes a sharp scolding noise and cuffs the little bears. She seems to say, "Come, come! Stop your play. There is much to see and do."

The cubs have already learned that they must obey their mother. If they do not they will be cuffed.

Mother Grizzly Bear is a good and loving mother but she is going to see to it that her babies are brought up as proper little bears should be.

The scolding brings Brother and Sister back to her instantly, and they follow her down the trail toward the valley.

Mother carries everything with her that she needs on a hunting trip. She has long, slightly curved claws on each of her five toes. With these she can rake and dig and fight. They are good tools and powerful weapons.

Her keen sense of smell tells her where to dig for roots and bulbs and burrowing animals. She can smell the faintest odor carried by the wind, and she can hear the slightest crackling of a twig. Her eyes cannot see very far, but her nose and ears serve her well.

Halfway down the mountain, Mother stops to sniff at a rotting log. Her nose tells her there are ants inside. With a powerful sweep of her paw, she rips the log open.

She places one paw on the angry ants. As they swarm up her leg she licks them off. Brother puts his paw on a heap of ants. They swarm up his leg and he licks them off.

A new sour taste fills his mouth. It is the good taste of ants. It is a taste bears like.

Mother turns over a big stone. She is careful to roll it to the side and away from her so it will not roll on her hind feet.

Underneath the stone she finds a nice meal of grubs and beetles.

Suddenly Mother Grizzly Bear rears up on her hind legs so she can see and smell and hear better. Danger is near!

A big Grizzly Bear, larger than Mother, is lumbering down the path toward them.

This is Father Grizzly Bear.

It is the first time Brother and Sister have seen him.

Father Grizzly Bear has spent the winter in a den of his own. He does not care anything about his children. He might even eat them if given a chance.

Mother knows this and is ready to defend her cubs, with her own life. She fills the air with terrible growls, angry snorts and sharp coughs.

Her loud, "Woof! Woof! Woof!" echoes through the mountains.

A warning growl sends the frightened little cubs scurrying into the bushes where they cannot be seen.

She turns toward Father Bear with teeth bared and her small eyes filled with rage.

Father Grizzly Bear looks at her for a moment and then turns and lumbers off toward the pine forest.

He knows, as do all the other creatures of the forest, that it is dangerous to fight with Mother Grizzly Bear when she fears her cubs may be harmed.

After so much excitement, Brother and Sister are tired and hungry. Poor little bears! They whimper like tired children. Mother leads them back up the mountain toward the den.

Going back, Mother steps in the same tracks she made when she came down the mountain, for that is the way of a bear. Stepping in the same tracks again and again will soon make a good bear trail.

Before they reach the den, a sudden gust of wind, a flash of lightning, and a low rumble tell of a coming storm.

Mother nudges the cubs with her nose and hurries them along. Already large drops of rain are falling.

Mother makes herself into an umbrella for the tired cubs. She pushes them underneath her, and straddling wide, she leads them safe and dry to the den.

The days come and go. Mother takes Brother and Sister farther and farther from the den. Every day they learn more about bear ways.

Sometimes they do not go back to their den at night. They find shelter beneath some drooping pine boughs or in a hollow place in the ground made by an uprooted tree.

They learn to strip the mountain berries from the vines. They do this by pulling whole branches through their mouths and chomping down berries, stems and leaves. They learn to dig for moles, ground squirrels and field mice. And they learn to swim in the cool mountain streams.

One day the bear family comes upon the carcass of a deer. What a feast they have!

Mother rips and tears the meat with her teeth and claws.

She has forty-two strong and useful teeth. She uses the ones in the front of her mouth for biting. On each side of these she has a big fang-like tooth which she uses for holding and tearing her prey.

Her back teeth have flat tops covered with ridges. She uses these for chewing and grinding the good deer meat.

The bears gorge until they cannot eat another bite. At last, full and happy, they lie down to take a nap.

The sleeping bears do not see a prowling mountain lion who comes slowly out of the spruce forest. It has smelled the deer and wants a share of it.

But Mother's ears and nose soon warn her of danger. Her loud "Woof! Woof!" again echoes through the mountains. She is suddenly changed into a savage beast with fangs and claws ready for battle.

Even the brave mountain lion does not care to fight Mother when she is guarding her food. It turns and slinks away. She might have crushed the mountain lion's skull with one blow of her powerful forearm.

Mother does not intend to waste a bit of the precious deer meat. She digs a shallow hole and covers what they did not eat with sticks and stones and dirt. They will come back another day to finish it.

But Brother and Sister are soon to learn that there is one enemy whom their mother fears.

In late summer they learn this. They are chasing grasshoppers in the meadow when they hear their mother's warning cough. They scurry back to her side.

Mother has caught a hated smell as it is carried up the valley by the wind.

It is the smell of man and his gun!

Mother knows that she cannot fight man and his gun.

She hastens to lead the cubs back into the thick forest. Quiet as mice, six bear eyes watch the man from their safe hiding place.

"No bears today," the man says, as he goes away.

All during the summer the Grizzly Bear family met few other Grizzlies. This is because there are no longer many left in the United States.

Before settlers came many Grizzlies lived peaceful lives in the western mountains. They were really shy and timid animals, who wanted to be left alone, as most wild creatures do. They did not lie in wait to attack either the natives or the settlers.

But the Grizzlies were feared by both because the bears were so big and strong and looked so fierce.

The natives' arrows could not kill the great shaggy bears easily. When wounded, and in pain, they attacked the natives.

The guns of the early settlers could fire only one shot which did not always kill the big bears, but only wounded them.

A wounded bear is a dangerous bear.

A mother bear defending her cubs is a dangerous bear.

And a bear defending its food is a dangerous bear.

When the Grizzlies stole a few of the settlers' cattle and sheep, they said, "We must kill all of these fierce Grizzlies."

At last a repeating rifle was invented which could fire many shots quickly. Now people could kill the bears easily. So year after year Mother Grizzly Bear's ancestors were killed until few were left.

Mother had learned that to flee and hide in the deep wilderness is her only chance to survive. Brother and Sister will learn this, too.

The days that follow are peaceful ones for this bear family. By now they have all stored many layers of fat under their shaggy coats.

Fat and happy, Mother, like all Grizzlies, enjoys sitting on a high place and looking out over the mountains and valleys. She enjoys, too, watching other wild creatures of the woods.

One day she takes Brother and Sister down to the stream to watch the beavers. They even stop their play to watch the beavers carrying sticks for their dam.

Father Beaver slaps the water with his flat tail as a warning to others. A beaver would make a nice meal for the bears, but food has been plentiful all summer and they are not hungry now. They are content to sit and watch the busy beavers.

In a few days each gust of wind brings a shower of red, yellow, and brown leaves to the ground. Many of the birds have gone south. Winter is on the way.

When the first snow swirls through the valley, Mother Grizzly Bear and the cubs climb the mountain and find their old den.

The snow drifts across the entrance to the den, shutting out the biting wind, and the three bears doze through the cold winter.

When spring comes again Brother and Sister have grown bigger. Now they do for themselves all the things they saw their mother do last summer.

They know about grubs and beetles that lie beneath stones. They know about the fat ants inside of rotting logs. And they know about burrowing animals that live underground.

They know about storms and changing seasons. And they know about people and their guns.

They are growing up. Mother pays less and less attention to them.

One day they see Father Grizzly Bear again. This time Mother does not growl at him. She seems friendly and willing for him to come near her.

Mother will have another litter of cubs during the coming winter. She may have two, or she may have three or four.

By late summer it is time for Brother and Sister to leave her so she can find a den where her new family will be born.

With Brother leading the way, they disappear into the thick pine forest.

Brother and Sister will stay together until they find mates and dens of their own.

THE POLAR BEARS

THE POLAR BEARS

Two little Polar Bear cubs follow their mother across the snow-covered land near the North Pole.

They look like little walking snowballs, with black-button eyes and black-tipped noses.

Mother Polar Bear makes big tracks in the snow but the cubs make little tracks no bigger than a silver dollar.

Walking through the deep snow is hard work for such small bears. Brother falls down in a snow drift and cries. Sister tries to comfort him.

Mother Polar Bear is a kind mother. She lets the tired little cubs climb up on her back for a piggy-back ride.

Hi! Ho! Away they go toward the open sea.

It is easy for Mother to carry her cubs on her back, for she is big and strong.

She wears a yellowish-white coat of heavy fur which keeps her warm in the cold Arctic weather. Her enemies, as well as the animals she wants to kill, cannot see her very easily because her coat is nearly the same color as the snow. Her nose and lips and eyes are black.

Mother Polar Bear's neck is longer than that of Mother Grizzly Bear, and her head is small and slender.

Of all the bears in the world, the Polar Bear family is the most beautiful.

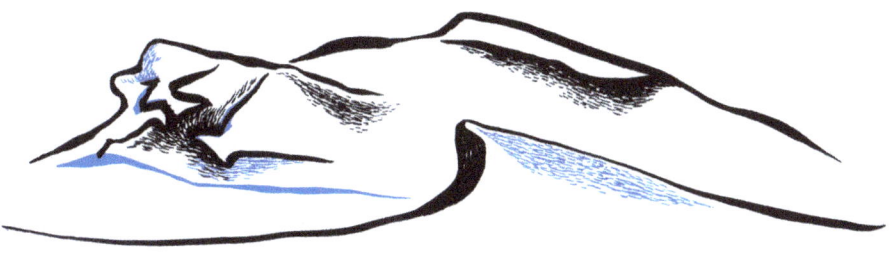

Before the long Arctic winter began Mother Polar Bear left her hunting grounds along the water's edge and came inland to make her winter home.

With her huge paws she scooped out a den in the deep snow. Down and down she dug. Then, curling up in the hole, she let the snow drift over her. The rising warmth from her body kept open a little breathing hole in the snow that covered her.

Mother Polar Bear drowsed in her snug white bed all during the cold, dark winter while the snow drifted deeper and deeper in the outside world.

Here, in January, the two little cubs were born.

Like their cousins, the Grizzly Bears, they were born with no teeth, and eyes shut tight. They were somewhat larger, but they did not weigh as much as *two* pounds of butter. Their pink skins were almost naked, but before long they were covered with snow-white downy fur. They opened their eyes and cut their teeth when they were about six weeks old.

The little Polar Bears grew much faster than human babies. Now, by mid-March, they are big enough to follow their mother as she returns to her hunting grounds near the water.

When, at last, they reach the Arctic Ocean, Sister and Brother Bear find that it is a noisy place.

Large pieces of floating ice crack and crash together with a noise like thunder.

The waves pound the icy coast with a booming sound.

And giant icebergs grind together.

Mother Polar Bear gives Sister and Brother their first lesson in catching seals.

She sees a sleek, fat one napping on the ice. But she must use every trick she knows to catch the seal.

She lies down on the ice with her front paws stretched out in front of her. Slowly and cautiously she pulls herself forward while her hind legs trail behind her. Inch by inch she moves toward the sleeping seal.

But the seal does not stay asleep for long. Up pops its head, and the seal looks around to see if its old enemy, the Polar Bear, is near.

Mother lies very still until the seal goes back to sleep again. Then she pulls herself forward as before.

But suddenly the seal raises its head and, this time sensing danger, quickly slides into a blowhole in the ice.

Mother knows it is no use to try to catch the seal in the water. It can swim faster than she can even though she is a powerful swimmer.

So she hunts and finds another seal. This time she is able to pull herself close enough to the seal while it is napping, so that, with a great rush, she pounces. She crushes its skull with one blow of her huge paw.

She rips the seal open with her claws and what a fine meal she has! It is the first food she has had since her winter sleep.

The Polar Bear family has great fun swimming and diving and twisting and turning in the icy waters. They play games in the water as other bears play on land.

Some people call them "Water Bears."

They are strong, graceful swimmers. Sometimes they swim with all four feet. At other times they paddle "dog fashion" with their front feet and trail their hind legs in back of them.

One day Mother lets Sister and Brother cling to her fur while she takes them for a fast ride through the water.

Mother Polar Bear has a much keener sense of smell than Mother Grizzly Bear. One day her nose tells her of a far off herd of walruses. She is hungry for a meal of baby walrus meat.

At length, they come upon a herd of white-tusked walruses on the ice. Mother is ready to pounce on Baby Walrus when Mother Walrus screams for help. Baby Walrus bleats in fear. What a noise they make!

Instantly the whole herd answers the call for help. With white tusks flashing, the awkward giants rush toward the bears. Mother Polar Bear knows that she cannot fight the whole herd. She quickly nudges the cubs ahead of her as she retreats.

As Sister and Brother grow older they swim far out across the rolling sea to the distant icebergs. One day, tired of swimming, they climb up on a large piece of floating ice to rest.

Looking out across the water they see handsome Father Polar Bear on *his* piece of ice.

Father Polar Bear is large, ferocious and brave. He fears no enemy except the Inuit and others who hunt him.

He is a great traveler. He wanders over many miles of ice and snow in his never-ending search for food.

He is the Monarch of the Arctic.

He is the Great Ice King.

Father does not den up in winter as Mother does when she is going to give birth to her cubs.

All during the long, dark Arctic winter, lighted only by the flickering flashes of the northern lights, he roams over ice and snow.

As all Polar Bears do, he wears fur overshoes on his travels. The soles of his feet are covered with stiff fur which keeps him from slipping on the ice.

He is a great meat eater. But if he can find grass, he will eat it too, as Grizzlies do. Sometimes he climbs the mountains on the islands, and there he digs for birds, called puffins, hiding in the crevices of the rocks.

He cares nothing for his children and leaves their upbringing to Mother Polar Bear.

Sister and Brother come to know White Fox and the Sea Gulls.

Day after day, White Fox follows the bear family and eats the scraps of seal meat which is left. When White Fox has eaten its fill, the hungry gulls swoop down and eat the last remaining bits.

White Fox cannot catch seals as the bears do. It might die from hunger in this barren north land if the Polar Bears did not provide the fox with food.

The fur traders killed many of Mother Polar Bear's ancestors. They killed the great white bears for their fur, which brought a good price in the market. At one time wealthy people used white bear skin rugs on their polished floors.

Inuit hunters kill the Great Ice Bear for both meat and fur. A fat bear feeds a family for many days, and the fur makes warm clothing and sleeping robes. Teeth and claws are used for ornaments and necklaces.

The fur traders also kill the white foxes for their fur, which brings a good price in the market. The traders have learned that the foxes would die if the bears did not leave food for them.

So laws have been passed to protect the bears. Now Mother Polar Bear need not fear as many hunters as her ancestors did.

Sister and Brother continue to hunt with their mother all during the short Arctic summer.

When the long, dark winter settles down they do not go back to the den as Grizzlies do. Like Father Polar Bear, they stay out in the bitter cold and hunt.

Sister and Brother stay with their Mother until they are about a year and

a half old. Now they are big bears. They weigh almost two hundred pounds.

Mother is free now to spend some time with Father Polar Bear. Then she again goes inland to dig another den. By the time Sister and Brother are two years old, Mother will be busy with a new family.

Someday Brother will find a mate with whom he will stay only a short time. Then, like his father, he will roam and hunt.

Sister, too, will find a mate and then go inland to dig a den and raise a family of her own.

THE ALASKAN BROWN BEARS

THE ALASKAN BROWN BEARS

Mother Brown Bear sits quietly on her great haunches in the snow near the entrance to her den in a rocky cliff.

She is still drowsy after her long winter sleep.

But her two little cubs are wide awake. They play hide and seek as they run in and out between their mother's legs.

They look like bright-eyed Teddy Bears come to life.

Suddenly, a dark shadow moves across the snow and a large eagle swoops down noiselessly from the sky. It sinks long talons in Brother Bear's wooly back and snatches him from the ground.

Brother shrieks like a human child. He arches his little back and twists and turns. At last he slips from the strong talons. Down, down, down he falls.

With a great cry of rage and fear, Mother Brown Bear rushes down the mountain.

She finds Brother in a snow bank. Only the top of his head and his little rounded ears show her where he is.

She digs him out of the snow and tenderly licks the wounds on his back made by the eagle's long, sharp talons. She makes comforting noises deep in her throat. Then she leads him back up the mountain and into the den.

Mother Brown Bear lives on the Alaska Peninsula. This is a piece of land that stretches out from the mainland of Alaska like a long arm.

Here there are volcanoes and snow-capped mountains. Little twisted trees of alder, dwarf willow, and pine grow on the lower mountain slopes in the valleys.

Fog rolls in from the Bering Sea. Cold winds and rain whip through the valleys. In this wild, rough country the biggest bears on earth have their homes.

They are the largest meat eating animals that live on land.

The are called the Giant Brown Bears of Alaska.

When Mother Bear stands on her hind legs she is taller than the tallest person. Like her near relatives, the Grizzly Bears, she has a hump on her shoulders and a dished face, but her claws are shorter and more curved than theirs. An Alaskan Brown Bear's coat can range from blond to a rich, dark brown.

Like all little bears, Brother and Sister Brown Bear were tiny, helpless creatures when they were born in January. Now they are as large as puppies and are ready to learn how to take care of themselves in this rough country.

When Mother Brown Bear first comes out of her den she eats only the red-tipped grass that grows above the timberline. But in a few days she grows hungry for the food that grows in the valley. She leads the cubs down the bear trail to the lowlands.

Remembering the eagle, she follows the trail that leads through the alders. Here the little cubs cannot be seen by enemies.

In the valley Mother eats skunk cabbage roots, a ground squirrel, many mice and some salmonberries. How good her first real meal tastes!

But Brother and Sister do not have a good time. Here in the lowlands, mosquitoes bite them and insects sting them. They bite and sting their noses. They sting their stomachs where the hair is thin. Oh, dear! There are swarms of insects everywhere.

Brother and Sister whimper and cry and rub their little paws over their faces.

When they go back to the home den they stretch out on the snow to rest. Here on the snow fields in the highlands there are no stinging insects to bother them.

As the days pass, Mother becomes restless. She looks out across the valley and swings her big head from side to side. She makes a deep rumbling noise in her throat.

Then, one day, she calls the cubs to her and hurries down the mountain.

Mother Brown Bear is going on a trip.

It is hard for Brother and Sister to keep up with her. When they lag behind she growls impatiently. They do not understand why she is in such a hurry.

As they travel onward they follow the streams that lead toward the sea. At night they sleep in soft moss-lined hollows in the ground.

They see foxes and rabbits and ptarmigan. They see a herd of caribou with slender deer-like heads. And they see the tracks of other bears.

All of the bear tracks lead toward the Bering Sea.

At last they leave the valley and come out onto the flat plain where the big river empties into the sea.

Here, wading about in the tall swamp grass, they see many other bears that have traveled down from the mountains. Big bears. Medium-sized bears. Little bears.

Noisy seagulls wheel and circle overhead. Terns and long-billed curlews, ducks and beautiful Emperor geese are gathered along the beach.

Above the chatter of the birds they hear the thundering waves of the stormy Bering Sea.

It is almost night and Brother and Sister are hungry. Mother finds a nest of gull eggs in the sand. With a tap of her big claw she opens an egg and eats the inside.

Sister tries to break open an egg but it rolls away from her. Finally she steps on it—hard! She gets only what she can lick off her spattered paw.

Brother licks the spatters off her face.

But they do not go to bed hungry. They drink their mother's milk until their small stomachs are full and round.

The next morning there is great excitement among the bears. They rear up on their hind legs and sniff the sea breeze.

It carries a delicious fishy smell.

All of the bears know that, at last, the salmon have come in from the ocean and have started swimming up the river to their spawning grounds, as they do every year.

It is feasting time for the Big Brownies!

Mother has arrived just in time.

Shuffling bears! Lumbering bears! Awkward galloping bears!

With eager, whimpering cries they all rush toward the river which is filled with the flashing silver backs of salmon.

Mother is the first to wade out into the river. With a quick snap of her powerful jaws she catches a wriggling salmon in her mouth and carries it to the shore. With her curved claws she neatly rips the flesh from each side of the fish.

Her big feast of the year has begun.

All that day and all that night the Big Brownies splash into the water and carry out the silvery salmon. Each eats their catch and then goes back for more until they are so full they cannot swallow another bite.

The seagulls flutter low, squawking impatiently for their share. They pounce on what the bears leave and pick the bones clean.

After the first big feast the brown bears do not act like such gluttons.

In the days that follow, Mother and Brother and Sister go down to the river in the morning for their catch of the salmon. When the midday sun is hot they rest in the alder trees. Late in the afternoon they return to the river for another meal.

The whole summer is spent fishing and sleeping and wallowing in the damp earth to escape the stinging insects. Toward the end of summer they start following the river back toward the home den. The bear family has stored enough fat to last them all winter.

One day Sister catches her first salmon in a shallow place in the river. But

before she can carry it to shore, Brother nips her. He wants the salmon for himself.

Sister forgets that her mouth is full. She opens it to nip Brother and away goes the fish!

Brother gets his ears cuffed playfully.

As the Brown Bears follow the streams back toward the home den they feed on late ripening berries.

Before long, cold fog rolls in from the Bering Sea. The leaves drop from the alders and the ferns turn brown. When the bitter November winds bring the first sleet and heavy snow the Brown Bear family hurries to their home den in the rocky cliff.

Here they sleep through the cold Alaskan winter.

Brother and Sister will probably be able to take care of themselves by the middle of the next summer. Some Brown Bear cubs, however, stay with their mothers until they are past two years old.

Each year Brother and Sister will travel to the Bering Sea for the big fish feast.

They will grow to be Giant Brown Bears of Alaska—and great fishers!

THE BLACK BEARS

THE BLACK BEARS

Deep in the evergreen forest in Maine the noisy Blue Jay calls, "Jay! Jay!"

Ruffed Grouse drums out its call on a favorite log.

The ice has melted in the woodland stream and its murmur fills the forest.

Mother Black Bear crawls out of the big hollow log where she has drowsed all winter. Two little wooly black cubs follow her on wobbly legs, like babies learning to walk.

They, too, were born during the winter.

If bears had birthday parties they would all be in January or February, for that is when all bear cubs are born.

Mother Black Bear shuffles down to the stream and has her first drink since wakening. The little cubs follow as best they can tumbling over sticks and stones like roly-poly puppies.

Mother Black Bear is the smallest of all bears that live in North America.

She has a smaller and more pointed head than the Grizzly or Alaska Brown Bears. Her face is straighter than theirs and she does not carry a hump on her shoulders. She has a brownish nose and a white spot on her chest.

Her claws are not as long as those of other bears. This makes her a good tree climber. Other bears can climb trees only when they are cubs, but Mother Black Bear can climb trees all her life.

But in one way her claws are like those of all the other bears—she cannot draw them in as cats do. This makes it rough to shake hands with bears.

Mother Black Bear takes the cubs along the stream where she digs for the bulbs of dog-toothed violets and lilies. She feeds on wild onions and the juicy stems of plants.

She finds dead May flies heaped along the stream and feasts on these. Like her relatives she turns over stones and rips open logs to find the grubs and ants. She digs for mice and moles and all the animals that burrow underground.

Sister and Brother Black Bear are prankish little cubs. Brother hides behind a tree and surprises Sister when he jumps out at her. They play "pretend." Sister pretends she does not see Brother and then suddenly turns and nips his round ear.

The game they like best is the "push-off" game. One climbs up on a rock and is pushed off by the other. What fun!

They play this game until they are so tired they drop down to rest, their stomachs flattened on the ground and their little legs spread out in all directions.

One day, while hunting in the forest, Mother Black Bear hears the barking of dogs, and her keen nose catches the smell of a human and guns. Her sharp warning cough calls the cubs to her and she hurries toward the stream.

She pushes the frightened cubs into the water. They must swim or drown. With Mother scolding and coaxing them, they paddle to the opposite bank. Here Mother sends them scampering up a tree.

They circle the tree with their small black arms, draw their hind feet up and under their stomachs and—push! Their sharp curved claws hold fast and up they go. Soon they are hidden among the leafy branches.

Mother follows them up the tree. From their safe hiding place they can see a man and his dogs. The dogs bark wildly for they have lost the scent of the bear tracks which lead into the water.

One day Mother finds some honey in a hollow tree. Sister and Brother dip their paws in the sweet, sticky stuff and lick it off. They have never tasted anything so good. But the angry bees swarm around their heads and sting their noses.

Sister and Brother slap at the bees and rub their stinging noses in the soft, moist earth. The cool earth eases their pain and back they go for more of the good sweet honey.

Before the summer ends, Sister and Brother learn a bear trick from Mother which all bears do except the Polar Bear.

She stands beside a tree and stretches up as far as she can reach. She claws and bites the bark, and leaves her mark of tooth and claw. She likes best to claw the aspen tree. The aspen tree will have these marks its whole life long, and all who see them will know that a bear has passed by.

It is said that other bears who see these marks will try to make ones higher. Just why they do this no one knows, but some people say that this is

the bear sign which says, "This is my hunting ground and you keep out."

The trees that have these marks are called "bear trees."

Even though Mother Black Bear has many Black Bear relatives, hunters seldom see them. Long ago they learned secret ways of keeping out of sight in the deep forests.

The early settlers killed them for their fat and furs and meat, and the bears soon learned to fear guns and traps. The settlers ate bear meat and used the furs for making robes. They used the fat for cooking, for soothing aches and pains, and for slicking down their hair to make them look more elegant. And to this day, the Royal Guards of England wear bearskin helmets.

Sometimes the early settlers had to kill the Black Bears because they stole their sheep and pigs. But many times cruel and stupid people killed them "just for fun," and not because of any need.

Wiser people have seen to it that many of the wild animals now have safe refuge in our National Parks. Here no gun may be fired and no traps set. Wise people know that our forests would be dull and lonely places if all wild creatures were allowed to be thoughtlessly killed.

Many of Mother Black Bear's relatives and many Grizzly Bears live in the National Parks. Here they do not run and hide for they are free from fear.

But Mother and Sister and Brother will remain wild bears, wise in the way of the forest.

Late summer finds them in the berry patches where Sister and Brother learn to strip the berries from the vines. They find blackberries, raspberries, wild strawberries, and wonderful plump blueberries.

They climb the trees for ripening beechnuts and acorns. When the first wild geese fly south and the maple leaves turn red, the Black Bears are ready for winter. They have stored plenty of fat and have grown heavy coats of glossy fur.

A driving snowstorm sends them hurrying to seek another hollow log for their winter home.

Next spring Sister and Brother will be husky bears. Mother will leave them to go her way and raise another family of little wooly cubs.

Sister and Brother will miss her for a while, but they will have each other until they find mates of their own.

www.ingramcontent.com/pod-product-compliance
Lightning Source LLC
Chambersburg PA
CBHW041326110526
44592CB00021B/2834